For Captain Raymond Holt.

He considered it.
He was interested.
He agreed to participate.

Quizzin' Nine-Nine

A Brooklyn Nine-Nine Quiz Book

Published by Beartown Press

Contents

Introduction

From Velvet Thunder (aka Captain Raymond Holt) to Billy "Big Time" Jankowski (aka Detective Jake Peralta), Brooklyn Nine-Nine has provided us with characters we've rooted for and storylines we've cared about for the best part of a decade.

It's more than just a comedy cop show; it's also touching, meaningful and important. And funny, so funny. That's why we love it and it's also why this quiz book exists. Please handle it with care, because you might find that it gets pretty hard, pretty quickly. (Title of your sex tape.)

Here's what you have on your hands:

- 360 quiz questions about Brooklyn Nine-Nine

- The questions are separated into 23 themed rounds, plus an extra set of tiebreakers to separate the Jakes from the jokers, and the Santiagos from the Santi-oh-no-nos

- Each round is made up of 15 questions (which is of course extremely fitting, because 15 is nine plus nine minus the square root of nine)

- Answer sheets for each round are located in the second half of the book

- If you haven't yet watched all of Brooklyn Nine-Nine, please be aware that this book contains spoilers (obviously)

So, if you're ready to prove who the most amazing detective slash genius is, let's get started...

NINE-NINE!

Season 1

1. What element of the precinct dress code is Holt keen to enforce on Jake during the pilot episode of Brooklyn Nine-Nine?

2. Who steps in as substitute when the Nine-Nine's usual criminal sketch artist falls ill?

3. While acting as secondary on a case where Boyle is the primary, Jake undermines his partner by taking over at the crime scene, but what other faux pas does he commit during that investigation?

4. In the pilot episode, Terry tells Holt that Jake "loves puzzles - in fact, the only puzzle he can't solve is…" what?

5. What is the name of the smartphone game which Holt and Gina become addicted to?

6. While attending Holt's birthday party, Charles meets and begins a relationship with Vivien. What is her occupation?

7. During Season One, Peralta and Boyle investigate a fire at Peralta's favorite pizzeria. Name that pizzeria.

8. And why is it Peralta's favorite pizzeria?

9. What is the name of the geeky, wannabe superhero who approaches the Nine-Nine to reveal information he has?

10. When Boyle is about to propose to Vivien, where does Jake drop the ring?

11. What is the full name of the black LGBT police organisation founded by Holt?

12. What is the name of the boyfriend Amy begins dating?

13. What is the name of the unhygienic co-worker who uses Rosa's desk on a different shift?

14. Which member of the Nine-Nine is sent undercover in the last episode of Season One?

15. Also in the final episode of the series, which two characters are shocked to discover they slept together?

Answers on page 54

Jake Peralta

Name a detective with more talent and less maturity than Jake Peralta. We'll wait. And while we wait, why not answer these questions about Jake?

1. What is Jake's favorite movie franchise?

2. And who is his favorite musical artist, who makes him "feel things"?

3. How long does Jake go undercover in the mafia for?

4. Jake began his career as a patrol officer with the 74th Precinct and was partnered with Stevie Schillens. What did the two nickname themselves?

5. What is Jake's mother called?

6. Who finds Jake and Amy kissing in the copy room and promptly dies?

7. What is Jake's traditional Thanksgiving food?

8. What was Jake's witness protection name?

9. What was Jake and Rosa's fitness-based promise system?

10. What is Jake allergic to, as revealed in Season Three?

11. What does Jake say is the moment he figured out he wanted to marry Amy?

12. What was Jake's prison nickname, given to him by Romero the gang leader in Season Five?

13. In contrast, what was Jake's high school nickname?

14. What does Jake claim to have legally changed his middle name to?

15. Who officiated at Jake's wedding to Amy?

Answers on page 55

Titles of Your Sex Tape

Can you tell which statements are "sex tapes" from the show, or made up?

1. "I came alone!"

2. "Kind, sober and fully dressed."

3. "Sorry, I thought that was a zucchini."

4. "They just sort of grabbed whatever and yanked."

5. "We need double the manpower on this immediately."

6. "That's not how holes work."

7. "I have to tell you, this is arousing suspicion."

8. "I hope it wasn't a mistake."

9. "Just a typical Thursday night in Wisconsin."

10. "A full-day team-building session *out* of uniform."

11. "I just got it out of the vent to rub it in your faces."

12. "Jake and Amy are getting married tonight."

13. "Any idea how long this thing's going to be?"

14. "There's a demon in our genes."

15. "She's coming - hide."

Answers on page 56

Amy Santiago

Sharp as a tack, unashamed nerdy and ambitious as hell, Amy Santiago's dream is to be the youngest officer to be promoted to captain. You know better than to bet against her, but what else do you know about her?

1. How many brothers does Amy have?

2. In Season One, Amy tells Terry that she and Holt are basically the same person. Name any three of the five characteristics she names that differentiate her from Holt.

3. Amy went to a weekend-long math conference in Season Four. What was its name?

4. What is Amy's favorite cop movie?

5. What stress-related addiction does Amy briefly have in Season Two?

6. Whose Wikipedia page did Santiago write? (Clue: they're a relative of a member of the Nine-Nine.)

7. What musical instrument did Amy play at school?

8. What animal is Amy allergic to?

9. What 'Most' was Amy voted in high school?

10. What risqué drinking game does Amy manage to ruin at her own bachelorette party?

11. Why is Jake's choice of wedding band a cause of awkwardness for Amy?

12. Which ceremony guest's dress does Amy get married to Jake wearing?

13. Which Broadway musical star guests as Amy's 'golden child' brother?

14. What rank is Amy promoted to in Series Five?

15. Amy tells Jake and Rosa that rules are made to be followed, not broken, and that nothing is made to be broken. Can you name any of the other four things they tell her are in fact made to be broken?

<u>Answers on page 57</u>

Season 2

1. Which crime family was Jake undercover to investigate before he returns to the Nine-Nine?

2. After which world leader are the "Jimmy Jab Games" named by Jake in Season Two?

3. Who is Boyle's date for his ex-wife's engagement party?

4. Who turns about to be the mole?

5. Who tries to teach Holt to cook for his anniversary breakfast?

6. Rosa meets a new love interest in the form of Captain Holt's nephew. What is his name?

7. What is Jake's dad's job?

8. In Season Two, Terry finds out his wife is pregnant with their third child. What do they eventually name her?

9. Who guest stars as Jake's love interest Sophia?

10. Which two characters get exactly the same score on a personality test?

11. How does Holt's office get ruined?

12. At the wedding of Gina's mother and Charles's father, who acts as minister?

13. And who loses the wedding ring?

14. What role is Holt promoted to (against his wishes) in the season finale?

15. Who engineers that promotion?

Answers on page 58

Rosa Diaz

Sword-owner, leather jacket enthusiast and the most fearsome woman in New York, Rosa Diaz is perhaps the one angry voice in the Nine-Nine. But how well do you really know her?

1. Which of the following did Rosa NOT attend: ballet school, hairdressing school, medical school, or business school?

2. In the pilot episode, Charles asks Rosa to a movie which Rosa says is terrible. What is that movie?

3. What does Rosa name her dog, originally bought for Charles?

4. In Season Three, why wouldn't Rosa donate blood?

5. In Season One, how many press-ups is Jake forced to do when him not trusting Rosa causes Doug Judy to get away?

6. What is the name of Rosa and Gina's secret bathroom?

7. Before her ill-fated wedding to Pimento, Rosa's three maids of honour compete to throw the best bachelorette party. Who does she declare the winner?

8. In the 2nd Halloween heist, what is the nickname given to Rosa?

9. What do Rosa's neighbours believe her name is?

10. Who was the first character Rosa chose to reveal her bisexuality to?

11. And what weekly family event with her parents is put on hold when Rosa breaks the news to them?

12. Rosa says that she doesn't ask people out. What does she do instead?

13. What is apparently notable about Rosa's 'formal' leather jacket?

14. What is Rosa's full first name?

15. What was the name of Rosa's favorite teacher?

Answers on page 59

Anagrams

Can you unscramble these fiendish acronyms to reveal the Nine-names?

1. Fry For Red Jets?

2. A Palate Jerk?

3. Maintained Pro?

4. Herd Cad?

5. Randomly Hot?

6. Entailing It?

7. Eve Hurl Tut?

8. Against Mayo?

9. Yo Dud Jug?

10. Bachelors Lye?

11. Rev Nick Zone?

12. Jelly Honk?

13. Lunchtime Waned?

14. A Riz Soda?

15. Cyclical Dutch Honks?

Answers on page 60

Terry Jeffords

A family man and linebacker both at home and at work, Terry Jeffords is a man-mountain built to love. Terry loves his wife and children. Terry loves his precinct. And Terry definitely loves yoghurt. But how much can you remember about him?

1. In the pilot episode, Terry and Holt briefly discuss Terry's old nickname from the One-Eight. What was his nickname in that precinct?

2. And what is Terry's other former and more flattering nickname from his time as a field officer, a persona who "takes bad guys to jail and bad girls to bed"?

3. Who is Terry's favorite author, who he's fortunate enough to meet in Season Four and hand his own book to in Season Five?

4. How many calories does Terry claim he needs to eat in order to maintain muscle mass?

5. What are the names of Terry's twin daughters?

6. What is Terry's favorite yoghurt flavour?

7. While working at the 65th Precinct, Terry was mocked after he claimed that an accomplice to a burglary they were investigating was who/what?

8. Which Asian country did Terry study in for a year, resulting in him occasionally speaking the language throughout the show?

9. What rank does Terry hold for the first seasons of Brooklyn Nine-Nine?

10. And what rank does he move to in Season Six?

11. What type of medical procedure does Jake help prevent Terry from going through with in Season Two?

12. In the same season, Terry creates a book for his daughters which features a pair of charcters based on two members of the Nine-Nine. Which two?

13. What exercise is Terry taking part in with Charles and Holt when he injures himself?

14. In the finale of Season Six, Terry is in denial over getting transferred to where, until Wuntch uses her temporary position to allow him to stay at the Nine-Nine?

15. Finally, what is the name of Terry's lovely wife?

Answers on page 61

Season 3

1. What tablet-like technology does new captain Seth Dozerman issue to the precinct in order to keep them motivated to accomplish something every 55 minutes?

2. How does Dozerman die?

3. Who replaces him as captain?

4. What degrading outfit does Wuntch force Holt to wear as part of his new role in the PR department?

5. Which serial killer do Jake and Holt bring to justice after ten years?

6. What sport do Holt and Boyle partner up to compete in?

7. What is the instrument of the "celebrity" musician whose case Holt allows Jake to join him on?

8. What is the alliterative name of the head of the custodians, who initially refuses to help the Nine-Nine with their garbage issue?

9. Season Three sees another precinct temporarily take up residence in the Nine-Nine's office due to a plumbing emergency. Which precinct is it?

10. Where does Cheddar run to when he escapes Jake and Amy's dog-sitting?

11. When Jake and Rosa catch a jewel thief, detectives from which European country join them to help track down the spoils?

12. How long is Adrian Pimento said to have been undercover for?

13. And what was the name of the crime boss whose gang he was undercover in for that time?

14. When Gina is preparing for her astronomy test, who does Terry bring in to help her study?

15. What is the name of Holt's former partner, who he brings into the fold to help the Nine-Nine infiltrate the FBI headquarters?

Answers on page 62

Charles Boyle

A man whose drive and detective work is rivalled only by his culinary passions, Charles Boyle is perhaps the biggest-hearted officer the precinct has in its ranks; almost puppy-like in the way he unconditionally loves and idolises the things he cares about, such as Jake. But how well do you know Mr Charles Boyle?

1. What is Charles's adoptive son called?

2. How does Charles meet his partner Genevieve?

3. In Season One, Charles judges a pie contest between two members of the Nine-Nine - who are they?

4. Reacting to Jake and Amy's first meeting (shown through flashback footage), what does Charles claim to hear?

5. For what heroic act was Charles awarded the Medal of Valor?

6. Much to his chagrin, Charles's rival receives the same medal in the same ceremony. What is the name of his nemesis?

7. What does Charles tell Jake is the Boyle's' family crest, while he's encouraging him to give up on trying to overturn his NutriBoom contract?

8. What is the one item sold from Boyle's food truck, The One Thing?

9. From Charles's perspective, what is unfortunate about the footage captured by Rosa's body cam as she takes down a criminal?

10. What variation on a famous *Die Hard* quote does Charles deliver when taking out a bad guy in the Christmas Eve hostage situation?

11. Which patriotic action figure does Charles go to extreme lengths to try to acquire as a Christmas present for his son?

12. What is the name of Charles's ex-wife, who holds his sperm to ransom?

13. And who did she cheat on Charles with?

14. Which incident in the line of duty left Charles sterile (or "shooting dust", as he puts it)?

15. Where is the ancestral home of the Boyles?

Answers on page 63

Halloween

It's the most important day of the year for any Brooklyn Nine-Nine fan. What can you remember about the Halloween heists?

1. Who wins the first ever Halloween heist?

2. What is the item targeted in the heist in the first ever Halloween episode?

3. And what are the stakes between Holt and Jake?

4. As of Season 5, what is the statement that the losing competitors must deliver to the winner?

5. True or false: Charles has won the Halloween heist?

6. What item does Jake have to steal from Holt in the second Halloween heist?

7. In Season Three, why do neither Jake nor Holt pick Amy for their respective heist teams?

8. What is the trophy in that third heist?

9. Who wins the fourth heist?

10. What scheme is Jake forced to invest in, in order to escape containment during the fifth heist?

11. What does Jake change the inscription on the champion cummerbund to in Season Five?

12. In Season Six, the Halloween heist takes place on which May celebration?

13. Which exam does Terry reveal that he has passed after securing the win at that heist?

14. Who wins the Season Seven heist?

15. How many times does that person technically win the heist during Season Seven?

Answers on page 64

Captain Holt

How much do you know about Velvet Thunder himself, Captain Raymond Holt?

1. What is the name of Captain Holt's dog?

2. And what is his husband's name? Bonus point if you can get his surname.

3. What is Holt's mother's occupation?

4. What is Holt's favorite color?

5. What does Holt tell Amy people mean when they say "What's up?"?

6. Who liberated Holt's pie from the office, which he was planning to take to a Thanksgiving party?

7. What physical pursuit causes Holt to hurt his wrist, a fact he shares with Jake because "no one will ever believe him"?

8. Since which year has Holt been an openly gay police officer?

9. Who was Holt's arch nemesis from his glory days, who he arrested while telling him to "drop the yoyo"?

10. What addiction has Holt battled in the past, which rears its head again in Season Five?

11. What is Holt's middle name?

12. What does Jake eventually work out is Holt's 'tell' when he's playing poker?

13. What game does Holt play against Gina for his 'special Gina moment' in the lead-up to her departure?

14. What name is Holt given when he and Jake enter witness protection in Florida?

15. To maintain his cover as a straight man, what does Holt claim is his favourite part of a woman?

Answers on page 65

Season 4

1. Where are Jake and Captain Holt relocated to for witness protection?

2. How do they manage to escape from jail after staging a fight between their fellow prisoners fails to spark any intervention from the guards?

3. In the manhunt episode, how many fugitives are on the loose?

4. Whose apartment do Jake and Amy move into?

5. Why is Amy unable to burn Jake's towel?

6. Which NFL player cameos as a particularly unhelpful witness?

7. In preparation for meeting Amy's dad, Jake compiles a binder on him that includes old photos of Mr Santiago with a ponytail that puts Amy's to shame. What does he say his nickname was?

8. And what does Mr Santiago's reciprocal binder reveal is Jake's credit score?

9. When Jake is using the alias Tyler Omaha to infiltrate a biker gang, what alias does Charles use for his roller-skating sidekick?

10. Where does Amy disappear to for some quiet time before her sergeant's exam?

11. Terry and Captain Holt compete to build the best *what* for the precinct lobby?

12. What possession of Amy's does Holt lose, allowing him to help her open up and express her anger?

13. How much money does Holt loan Pimento to help him get his PI license, only for Pimento to gamble on the dog show that Holt is watching on TV?

14. What is the name of the book franchise authored by DC Parlov?

15. The ex-partners of which two members of the Nine-Nine are assigned to audit the precinct?

Answers on page 66

Who Said It?

Time for a quickfire quotes round. Which characters first delivered these legendary Brooklyn Line-Lines?

1. "And if I may do a third toast, it'll be focused primarily on the mango yoghurt."

2. "I've only said 'I love you' to three people; my mom, my dad and my dying grandpa. And one of those I regret."

3. "I was thinking about how I would make the perfect American president, based upon my skill set, dance ability and bloodlust."

4. "I wasn't hurt that badly. The doctor says all my bleeding was internal. That's where blood is supposed to be."

5. "I'm playing Kwazy Cupcakes, I'm hydrated as hell, and I'm listening to Sheryl Crow. I've got my own party going on."

6. "This one says Die Pig. And worst of all, they didn't put the comma between die and pig."

7. "Can't spill food on your shirt if you're not wearing one."

8. "I work best alone. Except when it comes to sex. Actually, sometimes including sex."

9. "Preparing food for one's lover is the most intimate gift of all. Aside from washing their hair."

10. "If I die, turn my tweets into a book."

11. "Captain Wuntch. Good to see you. But if you're here, who's guarding Hades?"

12. "Anyone over the age of six celebrating a birthday should go to hell."

13. "First off, the name's Santiago. Detective Amy Santiago. Second, I'm arresting your son. Which, as I say it aloud, seems like an unwise choice, but it's the one I'm making. Once again, my name is Amy Santiago."

14. "I don't want to hang out with some stupid baby who's never met Jake."

15. "If we're away from our desks for too long, they'll update our computers and we'll lose Minesweeper."

Answers on page 67

Doug Judy

In another life, perhaps Doug Judy might have worked for the Nine-Nine, instead of being pursued by them for the majority of his time in the series. You wouldn't trust as far as you could throw him, but how well do you know Judy?

1. What is Doug Judy's crime nickname?

2. Who does Doug Judy manage to frame for his crimes in order to escape in his first Brooklyn Nine-Nine appearance?

3. What is the name of the drug being sold by the ring Judy helps Jake and Rosa to infiltrate in Season Two?

4. What does he also request that Rosa refer to him as, as part of his negotiations?

5. Where do Jake and Amy encounter Judy during Season Three while on vacation?

6. What is Judy working as there?

7. What is the name of Doug Judy's adopted brother, introduced in Season Four?

8. In exchange for Judy's help in catching his criminal brother, Jake offers him full immunity for all his past crimes. According to Holt, how many crimes is this, to the nearest hundred?

9. Granted immunity for his crimes, Judy buys Holt a new car. What does he name it?

10. In Season Six, what is Doug working as?

11. Despite going straight, Judy is forced by a violent drug dealer to carry out a diamond heist to avoid whose death?

12. At the end of that Season Six episode, Judy returns the diamonds from their heist to Jake and addresses him via a pre-recorded video, screened where?

13. Who is the copycat criminal carrying out car thefts using Judy's MO?

14. In Season Seven, whose private jet does Judy take to Miami for his bachelor party?

15. Who does Judy ask to be the best man at his wedding?

Answers on page 68

Season 5

1. Who was the ringleader behind the robberies Jake and Rosa were framed for and convicted of?

2. What is the name of Jake's prison cellmate?

3. What food item does Jake smuggle into prison in order to curry favour with Romero?

4. How is Romero moving the drugs into and around in prison?

5. Which mobster does Holt end up in hock to in exchange for the information that allows him to put away Hawkins?

6. What favour does that mobster call in as a result?

7. Which actor's movie catalogue do Jake and Kevin end up bonding over while the former is providing protection detail for the latter?

8. Why is Holt's Twitter account suspended?

9. When trying to infiltrate the NutriBoom conference, how does Charles ultimately manage to convince the other attendees he is Bill?

10. Who is the main investor in Charles's food truck business?

11. Who swoops in to book the only date available at Jake and Amy's dream wedding venue?

12. Who (or what) steps in to serve as ringbearer at Jake and Amy's wedding?

13. What do Amy and Gina spend the day doing while waiting for Rosa to return from an active shooter situation?

14. Reginald VelJohnson makes a cameo appearance at Jake's bachelor party, but which *Die Hard* character did he play?

15. A criminal arrested by Amy in the past plants a bomb at Jake and Amy's wedding venue. How did he know when and where the wedding was?

Answers on page 69

Hitchcock & Scully

Brooklyn would be either a little more or a little less safe without the Rocksteady and Bebop of the Nine-Nine. Probably the latter. But what do you know about Hitchcock and Scully?

1. What are Hitchcock and Scully's actual first names?

2. Which of the two held the all-time record for cases closed in the Nine-Nine?

3. Where does Scully say his parents accidentally left him when he was nine, resulting in him learning French?

4. Who manages to save the day by speedily re-assembling crucial documents to help track down Seamus Murphy in Series Five, Hitchcock or Scully?

5. What is the name of the chicken restaurant frequently visited by Hitchcock and Scully?

6. True or false - Scully always carries a comb in his shirt pocket?

7. How do Hitchcock and Scully help to escape the gang's capture in "Operation Beans"?

8. In Hitchcock and Scully's competitive sit-off with Rosa, who ends up leaving their seat first?

9. What is the name of Scully's twin brother?

10. In the pilot episode, Scully is introduced as "a bad detective who can ____ ____ ____". Fill in the blanks.

11. True or false: Hitchcock has appeared in more episodes than Scully?

12. What are Hitchcock and Scully's nicknames, occasionally used by themselves to refer to themselves?

13. What is the name of Hitchcock and Scully's van, where Jake discovers the missing fourth bag of money from their mafia boss takedown?

14. What did Hitchcock and Scully actually use the money liberated from the takedown for?

15. What is the name of Scully's dog and ex-wife (separate entities, same name)?

Answers on page 70

Complete the Quote

Fill in the blanks to complete these Brooklyn Nine-Nine quotes.

1. Charles: "You're without doubt the most incompetent detectives I've ever seen! And I'm including that bomb-sniffing dog who _____ _____ _____ _____."

2. Rosa: "What kind of woman doesn't have an _____?"

3. Captain Holt: "I wasn't injured; I was _____ _____."

4. Gina: "All men are at least 30% attracted to me. My mother cried the day I was born, because she knew she would never be better than me. At any given moment, I'm thinking about one thing: Richard Dreyfuss hunkered over eating dog food. I feel like I'm the _____ of people."

5. Wuntch: "Sticks and stones, Raymond." / Holt: "Describing your _____?"

6. Charles: "It's such a classic Boyle trait to not recognise talent. My cousin _____ didn't know she could sing until her late 40s."

7. Captain Holt: "She live tweets everything. Ruined _____ _____ for me."

8. Captain Holt: "You're Not Cheddar! You're just some _____ _____."

9. Jake: "Boyle, why don't you show Danger what a fax machine is."
Charles: "Okay. Imagine a letter had _____ _____ with a phone."

10. Jake: "The last movie she saw was a documentary about spelling bees."
Amy: "Wrong. It was about the font _____, and it played like an action thriller."

11. Jake: "All right, think. If you were Amy, where would you be right now?" Gina: "Oh, uh, boring pantsuit store. A crossword factory? A museum of retainers and headgear? Is it possible to enter _____ _____ _____?"

12. Captain Holt: "Here are two pictures. One is your locker, the other is a _____ _____ in the _____. Can you guess which is which?"

13. Gina: "Gina Linetti, the human form of the _____ Emoji."

14. Amy: "It'll cheer the captain up. He'll be over the moon. He may even lean back in his chair and _____ _____."

15. Captain Holt: "He was a great partner. Smart, loyal. Homophobic but not racist. In those days that was _____ _____."

Answers on page 71

Season 6

1. What is the name of the officer who is picked as commissioner over Holt?

2. Who is Amy dressed as while trying to convince a tied-up Holt not to resign from the Nine-Nine?

3. Where do Amy and Jake go for their honeymoon?

4. Why does Gina tell her mother to divorce Charles' father?

5. Holt, Terry, Hitchcock and Scully attempt to win a radio contest. What is the sound they are trying to recognise?

6. Nikolaj's birth father appears in Season Six. What is his name?

7. What dish do Hitchcock and Scully try to cook to perfection?

8. What is the name of Rosa's girlfriend, who she hesitates to introduce to Captain Holt?

9. Which group does the Nine-Nine challenge to a drinking contest to keep Shaw's as their hangout spot?

10. Who orders a sex book that's accidentally delivered to Amy's desk?

11. What anniversary is Jake and Gina's high school reunion celebrating?

12. What innovative punishment does Holt come up with for Jake's lateness?

13. What does Amy refer to as "nature's bullseye"?

14. Which three officers are recruited by Jake to form the 'Suicide Squad' required to take down the commissioner?

15. What job change is forced on Holt at the end of Season Six?

Answers on page 72

Cast & Crew

How well do you know the cast and crew of Brooklyn Nine-Nine?

1. Who plays Jake Peralta?

2. And who plays Amy Santiago?

3. Which two people created the show?

4. Where is the show shot? (Clue: it's not New York)

5. Who are the only two cast members to appear in every episode of Brooklyn Nine-Nine?

6. Who plays Doug Judy?

7. Which New Girl cast member appears in a brief crossover?

8. Who has directed every Brooklyn Nine-Nine series finale since Season Three?

9. Who was the first main cast member to direct an episode, in Season Six?

10. Which other two man cast members directed episodes that season?

11. Which cast member left as a series regular during Season Six?

12. Which of the cast originally auditioned for the role of Rosa Diaz before being cast as another character?

13. And which cast member originally auditioned to be Amy Santiago before being given a different role?

14. Who voices the Fremulon Productions credit after each episode?

15. Which network did Brooklyn Nine-Nine move to in 2019?

Answers on page 73

Peralta's Aliases

Can you tell the real Jake aliases from the ones we've made up?

1. Harvey Norgenbloom.

2. Herman the Janitor.

3. Detective Bart Barley.

4. Victor Silence.

5. Tony Wallop.

6. Carl "Mangy Carl" Mangerman.

7. Basil Chambers.

8. Vic Kovac.

9. Rex Buckingham.

10. Errol "Lofty" Lofthouse.

11. Dante Thunderstone.

12. Tyler Omaha.

13. Barry St. Barry.

14. Dr. Albrin Einstibe.

15. Reuben Vintage.

Answers on page 74

Gina Linetti

She moves in mysterious ways, so much so that you doubt whether anyone could ever truly know Gina Linetti. But maybe you can answer these 15 questions about her.

1. Gina fantasises about having her own fragrance line. What would it be called?

2. Gina keeps an intimidating jar on her desk at the Nine-Nine. What does the label say?

3. Which character went to the same school as Gina?

4. In *Halloween IV*, Gina uses a previous injury to her advantage. What is the injury?

5. What did Gina name her baby daughter?

6. Who is the father of Gina's baby?

7. Name either one of Gina's two dance troupes?

8. What is unusual about the dinner date Gina sets Rosa up with?

9. While the Precinct is under threat of being shut down in Season Four, "internet celebrity" Gina is pulling pranks on her colleagues for the benefit of her live audience (aka the G-Hive). What does she name her online portal?

10. Which character teaches (or attempts to teach) Gina to change a tyre?

11. What does Gina give Charles as a leaving present?

12. What does Gina say she would prefer to happen to her, than to read one of Charles's texts?

13. Gina claims to have met God when she dies for two minutes. What does she tell Rosa God looks like?

14. Which celebrity does Jake manage to get to attend Gina's leaving party?

15. What is Gina's actual job title at the Nine-Nine?

Answers on page 75

Season 7

1. Jake leads a manhunt in the season opener, but who did the huntee attempt to assassinate?

2. What does Jake find behind Captain Kim's locked door while trying to find evidence connecting her to Wuntch?

3. Who is trying to kill Adrian Pimento, as hinted at by a *Memento*-style tattoo?

4. Who wins the second edition of the Jimmy Jab Games?

5. Which two characters have a speed-reading completion while searching Debbie's diaries to help track her down?

6. What animal do Charles and Rosa raise a continuously-growing family of?

7. Whose final request was apparently for Holt to speak at their memorial?

8. What colour is the inside of the cake sliced open at Jake and Amy's gender-reveal party?

9. How do Jake and Amy eventually learn the gender of their child?

10. How does the vending machine selected by Hitchcock and Scully cause a blackout at the precinct?

11. What treasured personal item of Captain Holt's does Terry accidentally throw away?

12. Rosa competes against Teddy in an attempt to win what?

13. Who gets kidnapped by a gang leader in the penultimate episode of Season Seven?

14. What dish do Charles and Terry attempt to start a side business around?

15. What crucial ingredient does Terry leave out of the final recipe, resulting in a messy pitch?

Answers on page 76

Tiebreakers

Tied at the end of your quiz? Here are some "closest to" questions to help separate the wheat from the chaff.

1. As of the end of Season Seven, how many episodes of Brooklyn Nine-Nine have there been?

2. What year was Brooklyn Nine-Nine first broadcast?

3. What year was Andy Samberg born?

4. And when was Andre Braugher born?

5. How many Golden Globes has Brooklyn Nine-Nine won?

6. The show is partly shot in a real police station. Which real Brooklyn precinct actually uses it?

7. What is Jake's four-digit badge number?

8. On the Santiago Drunkenness Scale, how many drinks puts Amy at the 'A Little Bit of a Perv' stage?

9. How many years old was Jake when his dad walked out on his family?

10. How many times has Gina been engaged?

11. When Jake and Amy have a bet on which of them can get the most arrests, what is Amy's final score?

12. And what score does Jake post?

13. What date does Jake say he fell in love with Amy?

14. As of the end of Season Seven, how many episodes of Brooklyn Nine-Nine has Gina appeared in?

15. What year was Stephanie Beatriz born?

Answers on page 77

ANSWERS

Answer Sheet: Season 1

1. That he should wear a tie.

2. Terry.

3. He has "weird dead guy sex" with the forensic pathologist, causing a delay to the autopsy results.

4. How to grow up.

5. Kwazy Kupcakes.

6. She is a food author.

7. Sal's Pizza.

8. It was where his father took him after every Little League game he played as a kid.

9. Super Dan.

10. He drops it in a hotdog fryer of "boiling pork water".

11. African-American Gay and Lesbian New York City Policeman's Association (A.A.G.L.N.Y.C.P.A.). Catchy.

12. Teddy Wells.

13. Lohank.

14. Jake.

15. Charles and Gina.

Answer Sheet: Jake Peralta

1. *Die Hard.*

2. Taylor Swift.

3. 63 days.

4. The "Beatsie Boys".

5. Karen Peralta.

6. Captain Dozerman.

7. Mayonnaise and peanuts.

8. Larry Sherbet.

9. The 1000-push-up pact.

10. Bees.

11. When they were in bed together and Amy pointed out that there was a typo in her crossword puzzle.

12. "Beef Baby".

13. "The Tattler".

14. Sherlock.

15. Captain Holt.

Answer Sheet: Titles of Your Sex Tape

1. Sex tape.

2. Sex tape. Specifically, Jake's idea of Amy's sex tape.

3. Fake tape.

4. Sex tape. Boyle claims it is while talking to a coroner, who tells him that, at their office, sex tape is what they use to reattach a severed penis.

5. Fake tape.

6. Sex tape.

7. Fake tape.

8. Sex tape.

9. Fake tape.

10. Fake tape.

11. Sex tape.

12. Sex tape. Or, at least, Boyle claims it's the title of *his* sex tape.

13. Fake tape.

14. Sex tape.

15. Sex tape.

Answer Sheet: Amy Santiago

1. Seven.

2. "I'm younger, Cuban, female, single and straight."

3. "Funky Cats and their Feisty Stats".

4. *Training Day.*

5. She is addicted to smoking.

6. Laverne Holt.

7. The French horn.

8. Dogs.

9. Most appropriate.

10. Never Have I Ever, as she has never done anything embarrassing.

11. She used to date the lead singer and he's still in love with her.

12. Gina's. It sure was fortunate she was planning to wear a beautiful white dress to Amy's wedding...

13. Lin Manuel Miranda.

14. Sergeant.

15. Piñatas. Glow sticks. Karate boards. Spaghetti if you're using a small pot.

Answer Sheet: Season 2

1. The Ianucci family.

2. Mahmoud Ahmadinejad, President of Iran from 2005-2013.

3. Rosa.

4. Madeline Wuntch, with a little help from Lieutenant Miller.

5. Charles.

6. Marcus.

7. He is a pilot.

8. Ava.

9. Eva Longoria.

10. Holt and Gina.

11. Jake accidentally turns on the sprinkler with a rogue champagne cork.

12. Captain Holt.

13. Jake.

14. Head of NYPD public relations.

15. Captain Wuntch.

Answer Sheet: Rosa Diaz

1. Hairdressing school.

2. Citizen Kane.

3. Arlo. And she says she would kill anyone and then herself if anything happened to him.

4. She was scared of needles.

5. 2,000.

6. Babylon.

7. Charles. For letting her destroy things.

8. Dagger.

9. Emily Goldfinch.

10. Charles.

11. Games night.

12. She tells them where they're going.

13. It doesn't have any blood on it.

14. Rosalita.

15. Mrs. Weeniercool.

Answer Sheet: Anagrams

1. Terry Jeffords.

2. Jake Peralta. Pleasingly, he could also be 'A Jape Talker'.

3. Adrian Pimento.

4. Cheddar.

5. Raymond Holt. Fitting.

6. Gina Linetti.

7. The Vulture.

8. Amy Santiago.

9. Doug Judy.

10. Charles Boyle.

11. Kevin Cozner.

12. John Kelly.

13. Madeline Wuntch.

14. Rosa Diaz.

15. Hitchcock and Scully.

Answer Sheet: Terry Jeffords

1. Terry Titties. Because of his large... titties.

2. The Ebony Falcon. Except now the Ebony Falcon is monogamous and too tired for sex, so his only indulgence is fresh fruit yoghurt parfaits.

3. D.C. Parlov.

4. 10,000. That's a lot of yoghurt parfait.

5. Cagney and Lacey.

6. Mango.

7. A cat. Thankfully he and Jake went back to solve the case twenty years later. Turns out the cat didn't do it.

8. Japan.

9. Sergeant.

10. Lieutenant.

11. A vasectomy. Also the doctor didn't have an anaesthetic strong enough to take out a man of his size.

12. Amy and Gina.

13. Yoga.

14. Staten Island.

15. Sharon.

Answer Sheet: Season 3

1. "Dozerpads".

2. He has a heart attack after finding Jake and Amy kissing in the filing room.

3. The Vulture.

4. A pigeon costume.

5. The Oolong Slayer.

6. Squash.

7. He is an oboist.

8. Mean Marge.

9. The Nine-Eight.

10. The park where he and Kevin used to go.

11. Sweden.

12. 12 years.

13. Jimmy "The Butcher" Figgis.

14. Neil deGrasse Tyson.

15. Bob Anderson.

Answer Sheet: Charles Boyle

1. Nikolaj.

2. He is attending court at the same time she is being tried and eventually sentenced to ten years imprisonments for insurance fraud.

3. Rosa and Gina.

4. "Wedding bells!"

5. He leapt in front of Diaz when a criminal attempted to shoot her, taking two bullets to the butt.

6. Sergeant Peanut Butter, the horse.

7. A white flag.

8. The "perfect" meatball sandwich.

9. It also captures a fully nude Charles getting changed in the bathroom after he spilled pho on himself.

10. "Yippee-kayak, other buckets!"

11. Captain Latvia.

12. Eleanor.

13. Sleepy Stu, star of various mattress commercials.

14. While attempting to disarm a criminal he was bludgeoned in the crotch several times with a baseball bat.

15. Butt Thumb, Iowa.

Answer Sheet: Halloween

1. Jake.

2. Holt's Medal of Valor.

3. If Jake wins, Holt has to do Peralta's paperwork and call him his greatest detective; if Holt wins, Peralta has to work five weekends with no extra salary.

4. "[Winner] is the most amazing human slash genius."

5. False. Poor Charles.

6. His watch, a gift from his husband.

7. She is both Jake's girlfriend and Holt's mentee - neither believe they can completely trust her.

8. A commemorative crown.

9. Gina.

10. NutriBoom.

11. "Amy Santiago, will you marry me?"

12. Cinco de Mayo.

13. The Lieutenant's Exam.

14. Rosa.

15. Three - Halloween, Valentine's Day and Easter.

Answer Sheet: Captain Holt

1. Cheddar

2. Kevin Cozner.

3. She is a federal judge. Holt refers to her as "Your honor".

4. Tan. "It's no-nonsense".

5. They mean "I am a person not worth talking to."

6. Kevin, because "it was a horrible pie". Holt could tell it was Kevin because the pie had been placed down carefully in the trash - exactly how Kevin throws things away.

7. He was hula-hooping.

8. 1987.

9. The Disco Strangler.

10. Gambling.

11. Jacob.

12. He uses verbal contractions such as "I'm" and "There's".

13. Chess.

14. Greg Stickney.

15. The thigh gap, because "there's nothing more intoxicating than the clear absence of a penis."

Answer Sheet: Season 4

1. Coral Palms in Florida.

2. They kiss.

3. Nine.

4. Amy's. It sounds like it was a good decision. Jake only has one towel at his, and it was there when he moved in.

5. "Because it never fully dries".

6. Marshawn Lynch.

7. "The Lion".

8. 100. Out of 850.

9. Chip Rockets.

10. The rooftop when she and Jake had their first unofficial date.

11. Model railway.

12. Her pen.

13. $2,000.

14. *Skyfire Cycle.*

15. Amy and Terry.

Answer Sheet: Who Said It?

1. Terry.

2. Rosa.

3. Gina.

4. Jake.

5. Terry.

6. Amy.

7. Hitchcock.

8. Jake.

9. Charles.

10. Gina.

11. Holt.

12. Rosa.

13. Jake.

14. Charles.

15. Scully.

Answer Sheet: Doug Judy

1. Pontiac Bandit.

2. His barber.

3. Giggle Pig.

4. "Big Sugar".

5. On a cruise ship.

6. A lounge singer. He's actually surprisingly good.

7. George Judy.

8. 600.

9. "Sexarella".

10. He has become a high-end car broker, acquiring luxury vehicles for "the rich and famous" legally.

11. His mother's.

12. The karaoke club.

13. Trudy Judy.

14. Mark Cuban.

15. Jake, after he has arrested all of Judy's criminal friends at his bachelor party.

Answer Sheet: Season 5

1. Lieutenant Hawkins.

2. Caleb.

3. Ramen noodles (aka "street soups").

4. It's in the prison soaps.

5. Seamus Murphy.

6. He asks Holt to get a block party permit that will help cover up his gang's next crime.

7. Nicolas Cage. Although Kevin is angry when he learns Jake neglected to mention the existence of Cage's *Captain Corelli's Mandolin*.

8. The system identifies his robotic tweeting style as that of a bot.

9. By giving out Bill's patented neck massages.

10. Amy.

11. The Vulture.

12. Teddy's bomb disposal robot.

13. They (unsuccessfully) try to fix a toilet in the ladies' bathroom. Sadly they pretty much destroy it.

14. Sergeant Al Powell.

15. He saw an advertisement for the wedding which Charles had placed in the newspaper.

Answer Sheet: Hitchcock & Scully

1. Michael and Norm.

2. Hitchcock.

3. The Louvre.

4. Scully.

5. Wing Slutz.

6. False. Oddly, for a bald man, it's Hitchcock who does this.

7. Hitchcock manages to climb the stairs while tied to a desk chair, and Scully manages to sweat out of his restraints.

8. Scully.

9. Earl.

10. "Make good coffee."

11. False. They have appeared in the exact same number of episodes. That's nice, isn't it?

12. Flat Top and the Freak

13. Beaver Trap.

14. They gave it to the mafia boss's wife to help her start a new life when their boss wouldn't give her witness protection.

15. Kelly.

Answer Sheet: Complete the Quote

1. "Humps all the bombs."

2. "Axe."

3. "Lightly stabbed."

4. "Paris." If you happen to be single, reader, I would suggest using this quote as your Tinder profile.

5. "Breakfast."

6. "Susan."

7. "Downton Abbey."

8. "Common bitch." Poor old not-Cheddar.

9. "Unprotected sex".

10. "Helvetica".

11. "The color beige".

12. "Garbage dump in the Philippines."

13. "100".

14. "Nod slightly".

15. "Pretty good".

Answer Sheet: Season 6

1. John Kelly.

2. Holly McClane (neé Gennaro).

3. Mexico, funded by their wedding insurance payout.

4. Her mother was having an affair.

5. A bag of chips.

6. Gintars. He and Charles argue over the pronunciation of Nikolaj's name.

7. Lasagne.

8. Jocelyn.

9. The firefighters.

10. Terry, although he initially denies it to the point of getting his wife on speakerphone to confirm his skills under duress.

11. 20th.

12. He crafts an intricate high five with everyone in the office apart except for Jake, which he then proceeds to demonstrate.

13. A Colombian drug cartel member's nipple, after he is shot through it.

14. CJ, the Culture and Wuntch.

15. Wuntch forces him back to beat duty to make up for his missing patrol officer days, removing him as captain.

Answer Sheet: Cast & Crew

How well do you know the cast and crew of Brooklyn Nine-Nine?

1. Andy Samberg.

2. Melissa Fumero.

3. Michael Schur and Dan Goor.

4. Los Angeles.

5. Andy Samberg and Andre Braugher.

6. Craig Robinson.

7. Zooey Deschanel.

8. Dan Goor.

9. Stephanie Beatriz.

10. Joe Lo Truglio and Melissa Fumero.

11. Chelsea Peretti.

12. Chelsea Peretti (Gina).

13. Stephanie Beatriz (Rosa).

14. Nick Offerman.

15. NBC.

Answer Sheet: Peralta's Aliases

1. Real. CPA, recently divorced father of two with a dark sexual secret.

2. Real.

3. Real. Bart is tightly-wound and hates violence against animals.

4. Fake.

5. Fake.

6. Real.

7. Fake.

8. Real. Ex-Navy SEAL who got double-crossed and left for dead.

9. Real. British secret agent, ballistics expert, and ladies' man.

10. Fake.

11. Real. Stole his first car at the tender age of nine.

12. Real. BMX rider.

13. Real.

14. Real.

15. Fake.

Answer Sheet: Gina Linetti

1. *Gina in a Bottle.*

2. "Ashes of problem employees".

3. Jake.

4. Her missing two front teeth. (She lost them during the 5th minute of 7 Minutes in Heaven when a bowling ball fell on her face.)

5. Enigma (or Iggy for short).

6. Boyle's cousin, Milton (played by Ryan Phillippe).

7. Floorgasm and Dance-y Reagan.

8. The person she's actually setting Rosa up with is the bartender, not the annoying girl she's on the date with.

9. Ginazon.

10. Amy.

11. The Boyle family mother dough starter.

12. She claims she'd prefer to be hit by a bus. The irony…

13. "Ethnically ambiguous."

14. Mario Lopez.

15. Administrator.

Answer Sheet: Season 7

1. The city councillor.

2. Captain Kim's angry dog.

3. His doctor.

4. Jake.

5. Amy and Holt. (Charles is also there but speed reading is not his strong suit.)

6. Guinea pigs.

7. Madeline Wuntch.

8. Green. Roger and Walter messed up the baking of the substitute cake after ruining the first one.

9. Scully accidentally eats their replacement-replacement cake and enters the room with blue frosting covering his mouth.

10. It contains a pizza oven, and the outlet can't support the voltage.

11. A business card with a bit of gum stuck to it - the card belonged to the victim from Holt's first case, which he was never able to solve.

12. The elite baby stroller Amy wants.

13. Cheddar.

14. Charles's "bone broth".

15. Salt.

Answer Sheet: Tiebreakers

1. 143.

2. 2013.

3. 1978.

4. 1962.

5. Two, for Best Television Series and Best Actor in a Television Series (Andy Samberg).

6. The 78th.

7. 9544.

8. Four.

9. Seven years old.

10. Eight times.

11. 84.

12. 93.

13. April 28th.

14. 117.

15. 1981.

Made in the USA
Monee, IL
02 December 2020

50611587R00049